Understanding Love

Adrian Collins

Adrian Collins

Adrian Collins

Copyright Page

First edition
All Rights Reserved
Author: © 2024, Adrian Collins

Index

Adrian Collins

The Brain in Love

The brain is the real command center when it comes to love. Although we tend to associate romantic emotions with the heart, the reality is that everything we feel when we fall in love happens in our mind. Understanding how the brain works in these cases is not only fascinating, but it also helps us better understand why we do what we do in the name of love.

When we fall in love, our brain experiences a kind of "chemical storm." It all starts with dopamine, a neurotransmitter known as the reward molecule. When we are around the person we are attracted to, the brain releases dopamine in large quantities, making us feel euphoric, full of energy, and obsessed with being around that person. It is as if our brain rewards us every time we think or interact with that special person. That is why, in the early stages of love, it is common to feel like we can't get that person out of our heads.

Along with dopamine, there is another substance that plays a key role: oxytocin. Often called the love hormone, oxytocin is released in moments of emotional closeness or physical contact, such as hugs, kisses, or even a simple caress. This hormone strengthens the emotional bond between two people and creates a sense of trust and security. In romantic relationships, oxytocin is crucial for building deep and lasting connections.

On the other hand, norepinephrine, a chemical that activates our nervous system, also comes into action. This substance makes us feel more alert, attentive, and focused on the person we are attracted to. This is why we remember in such detail the little things, like what they were wearing or what they said at a specific moment. In addition, this chemical is responsible for the nerves and excitement we feel when we are around someone we like.

However, not everything is rosy. In this initial stage of falling in love, there is another part of the brain that works less: the prefrontal cortex, responsible for judgment and rational decision-making. Basically, when we are in love, our brain puts on "rose-colored glasses" that make us see only the good in the other person, ignoring their flaws or potential problems. It is as if our brain wants to make sure that we commit to that person without thinking too much about the risks.

As a relationship progresses, other parts of the brain begin to take center stage. Instead of relying solely on dopamine and initial euphoria, longer, more mature relationships are fueled by chemicals like serotonin, which stabilize our mood, and more oxytocin, which strengthens the emotional connection. This explains why long-term relationships feel less exciting in terms of intensity, but deeper and more rewarding.

In addition to chemicals, certain brain structures are also important in love. For example, the limbic system, which includes the amygdala and hippocampus, is responsible for processing our emotions and memories. These areas work intensely when we are in love, creating positive associations between the person we love and the moments we shared with them. So when we hear a song that reminds us of someone special or we return to a place where we spent time together, our brain activates those memories and floods us with emotions.

Love also has a complex relationship with fear. The amygdala, which is responsible for processing fear and anxiety, can be more active if we have had negative experiences in the past, such as painful breakups or betrayals. This can lead us to feel insecurities even when we are in a healthy relationship. Understanding this helps us recognize that some of our worries are not always related to current reality, but to emotional wounds that we have not yet healed.

The brain in love doesn't just seek immediate pleasure or reward. It also has an evolutionary purpose: to ensure the survival of our species. When we fall in love, the brain pushes us to form strong bonds that, in biological terms, ensure that we work as a team to raise children and keep them safe. Although our modern relationships are not always based on this need, the brain still operates with these "ancient instructions."

Knowing these processes allows us to be more aware of how our emotions and behaviors are influenced by brain chemistry. This doesn't mean that love is any less magical or meaningful, but it does give us tools to understand why we feel the way we feel and how we can manage our relationships in healthier ways. Ultimately, knowing how the brain works in love allows us to more fully enjoy the experience and build stronger bonds with the people we love.

Chemistry of Love

Love is not just felt; it is also produced, literally, in an internal laboratory within us: our body. The chemistry of love is a complex dance of hormones and neurotransmitters that work together to create the emotions, sensations, and behaviors we associate with being in love. Even though we can't see this chemistry, we experience it intensely in every glance, hug, or thought about that special person.

It all starts with dopamine, the substance that kick-starts our sense of happiness and reward. When we meet someone we are attracted to, the brain releases dopamine in large quantities, especially if that person responds positively. This neurotransmitter is to blame for making us feel euphoric, like we are on top of the world, whenever we are around that person or even when we simply think about them. It is for this reason that love can feel like a kind of "addiction." Our brain literally seeks out more interactions to get that dose of pleasure and satisfaction that dopamine provides.

Alongside dopamine, norepinephrine comes into play, another chemical that heightens our senses and emotions. This substance makes us feel alert, excited and full of energy, which explains why, at the beginning of falling in love, we often have trouble sleeping or eating. Norepinephrine also increases our ability to remember details related to the person we are interested in, such as what they were wearing or what they said in a seemingly trivial conversation. It is as if our brain is creating a detailed file on that person, preparing to strengthen the bond.

Oxytocin, known as the love hormone, is another protagonist in this story. It is released during moments of physical contact, such as hugs, caresses, kisses, and even during sex. This hormone not only creates a sense of connection and trust, but it also strengthens the emotional bond between two people. The more time we spend around someone, the more oxytocin we release, cementing the bond we share. This is why physical contact is so important in romantic relationships; it not only feels good, but it literally connects us on a chemical level.

Of course, we can't talk about the chemistry of love without mentioning serotonin. Interestingly, this substance, which regulates our mood, tends to decrease during the early stages of falling in love. This may sound counterintuitive, but it explains why we often find ourselves obsessed with our crush, constantly thinking about them. With less serotonin in the brain, it's harder to maintain a balanced perspective, leading us to focus our attention almost exclusively on that person.

Another substance that plays an important role, especially in long-term relationships, is vasopressin. This chemical is linked to commitment and loyalty. It is released during moments of physical and emotional intimacy, helping to consolidate the bond in the long term. Vasopressin is especially important in stable relationships, as it reinforces the desire to care for and protect our partner.

It is interesting to note that the chemistry of love can also be the reason for some irrational behaviors. During the early stages of falling in love, activity in the amygdala, the part of the brain that regulates fear and risk assessment, decreases. This makes us more likely to make impulsive decisions, such as idealizing the loved one or ignoring warning signs. Our brain, in its effort to foster bonding, literally puts us in a state where everything seems more positive than it really is.

There's also a less romantic but equally important role played by endorphins. These chemicals, known as the body's natural painkillers, help us feel relaxed and happy in the presence of our partner, especially in long-term relationships. Over time, endorphins replace some of the initial intensity of dopamine, creating a feeling of comfort and security that characterizes mature relationships.

The chemistry of love doesn't just affect our brains; it also has a physical impact on our bodies. For example, the surge of dopamine and norepinephrine can cause our hearts to beat faster, our palms to sweat, or even cause us to feel butterflies in our stomach. These physical effects aren't accidental; they're the result of a biological response designed to prepare us for emotional connection.

It's important to remember that the chemistry of love isn't permanent. The high doses of dopamine and norepinephrine we feel at the beginning don't last forever, and this is completely normal. Over time, love evolves, and oxytocin, vasopressin, and endorphins take over, creating a deeper, more stable bond. Although this may seem less exciting, it's what allows relationships to be long-lasting and meaningful.

Understanding the chemistry of love helps us demystify some of the emotions we experience and accept that we can't always control how we feel. However, it also reminds us that although love has a biological basis, our choices, attitudes, and behaviors are just as important in building and maintaining a healthy relationship. Ultimately, the chemistry of love is just the beginning; what we do with those emotions is up to us.

Emotional Attachment

Emotional attachment is one of the fundamental pillars of love and human relationships. It is that deep connection we feel towards someone, which makes us want to be close, share important moments and support each other. Although attachment is experienced in the heart, its origin is in our mind, where the strongest and most lasting emotional bonds are generated.

Emotional attachment begins to form as babies. From the moment we are born, our brains are programmed to seek closeness and security from the people who care for us. This is not only an emotional need, but also a matter of survival. A baby who forms a secure attachment with his parents or caregivers is more likely to receive protection, nourishment, and comfort, essential elements for his development. This early attachment pattern lays the foundation for how we form emotional relationships later in life.

As adults, emotional attachment works in a similar way, although it is now more closely related to our romantic partners. In a relationship, attachment is built through trust, intimacy, and consistency. Every time our partner responds positively to our emotional needs, our brain releases oxytocin, also known as the bonding hormone. This chemical strengthens our emotional connection and makes us feel safe and valued in the relationship. Over time, these repeated experiences create a strong bond that emotionally ties us to that person.

However, not all attachment experiences are the same. There are different attachment styles that affect how we relate to others. For example, people with a secure attachment tend to feel comfortable with closeness and intimacy, and trust that their emotional needs will be met. On the other hand, those with an anxious attachment may feel a constant fear of abandonment or worry excessively about whether their partner loves them enough. In contrast, people with an avoidant attachment tend to maintain a certain emotional distance, preferring not to be overly dependent on others.

These attachment styles are not accidents; they are deeply influenced by our childhood experiences. If we grew up in an environment where our emotional needs were consistently met, we are more likely to develop a secure attachment. But if our needs were ignored, rejected, or met unpredictably, we may develop more anxious or avoidant attachment styles. The important thing here is to understand that although our past influences the way we relate, it does not define us. With awareness and personal work, we can change the way we experience and express emotional attachment.

Emotional attachment not only binds us to our partner, but it also helps us regulate our emotions. In a healthy relationship, the presence of our partner can calm us in times of stress or anxiety. This is because our brain associates that person with security and comfort. It's as if, when we're with someone we're emotionally attached to, our nervous system automatically relaxes. That's why, after a tough day, a hug from our partner can have such a powerful effect.

However, emotional attachment can also have its tricky side. When we are too attached to someone, we may feel like our happiness is completely dependent on them. This can lead to unhealthy behaviors, such as emotional dependency, excessive jealousy, or a constant fear of losing our partner. This type of attachment is not the result of love itself, but of internal insecurities that need to be addressed. It is essential to find a balance where we can love someone deeply without losing our own identity or emotional well-being.

An interesting aspect of emotional attachment is how it evolves over time. At the beginning of a relationship, attachment is often full of excitement and intensity, fueled by dopamine and novelty. But as the relationship matures, attachment becomes more stable and comforting, thanks to oxytocin and endorphins. This doesn't mean that love disappears, but rather that it changes form, moving from the excitement of the initial stage to the security and trust of a deeper relationship.

It's important to note that emotional attachment doesn't mean being glued to your partner 24/7. In fact, a healthy attachment includes space and autonomy.

It's in that balance between closeness and independence that relationships truly flourish. When both people can be themselves while still trusting that the other will be there when they need it, attachment becomes a source of strength and mutual support.

To strengthen emotional attachment in a relationship, it is essential to cultivate moments of authentic connection. This can include simple activities such as chatting without distractions, sharing a hobby, or simply spending time together enjoying each other's company. Additionally, showing physical affection, such as hugs or caresses, is also a powerful way to strengthen the bond. The most important thing is to be emotionally present and available, showing our partner that they are a priority in our lives.

Emotional attachment is an essential part of love, but it's also a skill we can learn and improve. By understanding how it works in our minds and in our relationships, we can work to build stronger, healthier, and more meaningful connections. Because, in the end, attachment isn't just a feeling; it's a daily choice to care for, value, and be there for the person we love.

The Impact of Past Experiences

The impact of past experiences on our current relationships is immense, even if we sometimes don't realize it. From childhood to adulthood, all the important interactions we have had, especially the most significant or painful ones, leave traces in our minds and in our way of relating to others. These experiences shape our expectations, our emotional reactions, and the way we bond with the people we love.

From a young age, we learn what love feels like and how it is expressed by observing and experiencing the relationships in our environment. If we grew up in a home where there was affection, care, and communication, we likely developed a positive view of love and an ability to trust others. On the other hand, if our experiences were ones of abandonment, rejection, or constant conflict, these may have become patterns that we keep repeating without even realizing it. Our mind stores these memories as a kind of unwritten manual on how relationships work, and that manual can influence how we behave as adults.

For example, a person who grew up in an environment where affection was only given under certain conditions may have learned that love is earned, not given unconditionally. This might lead them to try too hard in their relationships, constantly fearing that if they don't try hard enough, they will be abandoned. In contrast, someone who experienced rejection might build emotional walls, protecting themselves from pain by avoiding deep connections with others. These behaviors are not conscious decisions, but rather learned responses that the brain uses to try to avoid repeating past suffering.

Romantic relationships, in particular, often trigger these past imprints in a powerful way. This happens because love touches our deepest emotions and awakens needs for connection and security that originated in childhood. This is why we sometimes react in ways that seem exaggerated or even irrational to certain situations in a relationship. For example, feeling emotionally abandoned, even temporarily, can unconsciously remind us of times when we felt alone or unprotected in the past, and our reaction can be much stronger than the current situation warrants.

A key aspect of the impact of past experiences is how they influence our choices in partners. Often, without realizing it, we seek out people who reflect familiar patterns, even if those patterns are unhealthy. This happens because our brain seeks out what is familiar, even if it is not always what is best for us. Thus, we can end up in relationships that repeat dynamics from the past, such as seeking emotionally distant partners because we grew up with parental figures who showed us no affection, or being attracted to conflict-ridden people because chaos was a constant in our childhood.

Furthermore, our past experiences not only shape how we choose our partners, but also how we interpret their actions. For example, if someone has betrayed us in the past, we might be more likely to distrust them, even when there is no apparent reason to do so. This emotional filter can distort reality and generate conflicts that are actually born from our internal wounds, not from our partner's actions. It's as if we carry an invisible backpack full of memories and emotions that influence how we perceive each interaction.

However, the impact of past experiences is not set in stone. While we can't change what happened to us, we can change how it affects our current lives. The first step is to become aware of those patterns and recognize how our past experiences may be influencing our relationships. This process requires honesty with ourselves and sometimes the support of a therapist or guide to help us safely explore those wounds.

Once we identify those patterns, we can begin to work on them. This may involve learning to distinguish between emotions from the present and those from the past, so that we don't react automatically to situations that remind us of old wounds. It also involves practicing self-acceptance and self-care, giving ourselves the love and validation we may not have received in the past. When we do this, we stop looking to our partners for what we couldn't get before, freeing them from impossible expectations.

Another important step is to communicate openly with our partner about our experiences and how they may influence our reactions. Sharing our vulnerabilities not only strengthens the bond, but it also helps our partner understand us better. For example, if we explain that a certain attitude reminds us of a painful situation from the past, he or she is more likely to be able to support us in an understanding way rather than feeling attacked or confused.

It is crucial to remember that our past experiences do not define us. We are more than our wounds and our memories. Every day, we have the opportunity to choose how we want to live and relate. This does not mean ignoring the past, but rather integrating it as part of our history, without allowing it to control our present. By working on our wounds and patterns, we can build healthier, more fulfilling relationships, based on love and genuine connection, rather than inherited fears and insecurities.

The impact of past experiences on our relationships can be profound, but it is also a doorway to growth and healing. By facing these influences with courage and self-compassion, we not only improve our relationships, but we also move closer to the most authentic and free version of ourselves. Because, in the end, love is not just about sharing our lives with someone else, but about learning to love and heal together.

Adrian Collins

What Makes Us Choose Someone?

What makes us choose someone as our partner? This question has intrigued psychologists, scientists, and poets for centuries. While it may seem like our romantic choices are completely spontaneous or guided by fate, the reality is that behind every attraction there is a complex combination of psychological, biological, and social factors that influence our decision. Understanding these dynamics is not only fascinating, but it also allows us to make more conscious decisions about our relationships.

One of the first factors that determines who we choose is familiarity. We tend to be drawn to people who seem familiar to us in some way, either because they share characteristics with those around us in our childhood or because they remind us of positive experiences from the past. This doesn't necessarily mean we're looking for someone identical to our parental figures or childhood friends, but there may be certain qualities or behaviors that make us feel at home. Familiarity breeds comfort, and that creates a foundation for connection.

Physical attraction also plays a role, though it's not as superficial as it may seem. It's not just about whether someone is "good-looking" by societal standards, but how certain physical features resonate with our personal preferences. This can include everything from eye color or tone of voice to the way someone smiles. Interestingly, physical attraction is also influenced by biological cues, such as those related to the immune system. Research has shown that we tend to be attracted to people whose immune systems are different from our own, which could be an evolutionary advantage for having healthier children.

Another crucial aspect is compatibility in values and personality. We look for people who share our goals, beliefs, and lifestyles, because this makes it easier to connect and reduces conflict. If someone values honesty, family, and stability, they are more likely to be attracted to people who share those same values. However, compatibility does not mean that both people are exactly the same. In fact, some differences can be attractive because they complement us, but those differences must be manageable and not go against what we consider essential for our happiness.

Emotional chemistry is another factor that we cannot ignore. There are people with whom we simply feel comfortable from the first moment, as if we could be ourselves without filters or pretensions. This emotional connection can be the result of how that person listens to us, understands us, and responds to our needs. For example, someone who is attentive and shows genuine interest in us can make us feel valuable and special, which strengthens the emotional attraction.

Context and circumstances also play a significant role. Often, our romantic choices are influenced by where we are in life. If we are in a stable stage and looking for commitment, we are likely to be attracted to someone with similar goals. On the other hand, if we are in a stage of adventure and exploration, we might lean toward someone who shares that free spirit. Additionally, proximity matters too; we tend to fall in love with people we interact with frequently, such as coworkers, friends, or neighbors.

A less obvious but very powerful factor is reciprocity. We are attracted to people who make us feel that they like us. This phenomenon is based on a basic need to be accepted and valued. When someone shows interest in us, our self-esteem rises and, as a result, we may begin to see that person in a more attractive light. It is as if the simple fact of feeling loved opens us up to the possibility of loving.

Past experiences also shape our choices. If we've had relationships in the past that left a positive mark on us, we're likely to seek to repeat those patterns. For example, if we were once with someone who made us laugh and felt safe, we might look for similar characteristics in future partners. However, negative experiences also play a role. If someone hurt us deeply, we might avoid certain personalities or behaviors that we associate with that pain, even if this isn't always conscious.

Idealization is another element that plays a role in our choices. Often, we project our expectations and desires onto a person, seeing them not only for who they are, but also for who we think they could be. This can be both positive and dangerous. On the one hand, it allows us to see the potential in someone and feel hopeful about the relationship. On the other hand, if our idealization doesn't align with reality, we can end up disappointed when the person doesn't meet our expectations.

It's important to mention that our choices are also influenced by society and culture. Beauty standards, gender roles, and societal expectations about what an ideal relationship is all affect our perception of what we're looking for in a partner. For example, someone may feel pressured to look for a partner who meets certain characteristics because that's what's considered "right" in their environment, even though it's not what they really want.

In the end, what makes us choose someone is a combination of conscious and unconscious factors that interact in a unique way in each person. The most important thing is to recognize that, although many of these elements are beyond our control, we have the ability to reflect on our decisions and make them more conscious. By understanding why we are attracted to certain people, we can make better decisions that lead us to healthier and more satisfying relationships. Because choosing someone is not only an act of attraction, but also an act of commitment to ourselves and to what we really need to be happy.

The Myth of Romantic Love

Romantic love is one of the most deeply rooted ideas in our culture, but also one of the most misleading. From a young age, we are surrounded by stories, songs, and movies that present us with an idealized version of love, as if it were a fairy tale where happiness depends on finding a perfect person. This concept, although inspiring, can be a dangerous trap, because it creates unrealistic expectations that affect our relationships. To understand love in a healthier way, it is essential to debunk the myth of romantic love and see it for what it really is: a cultural construct that does not always reflect reality.

Romantic love makes us believe that there is a "better half," a person predestined to complete us and make our life perfect. This idea can be comforting, but it also puts enormous pressure on us. Thinking that we will only be complete by finding someone special can lead us to feel incomplete while we are alone. In addition, it puts the responsibility of making us happy on our partners, as if they were the solution to all our internal problems. The reality is that no one can fill us with happiness if we are not okay with ourselves first.

Another problem with the myth of romantic love is that it promotes the idea that relationships must be perfect. According to this narrative, if there are arguments, differences, or moments of boredom, then the relationship is not "the right one." But this is far from the truth. All relationships have challenges. Arguments are normal and, in fact, necessary to resolve problems and grow as a couple. Believing that true love is always easy can lead us to give up too quickly when we face difficulties, rather than working to improve the relationship.

The myth also idealizes intense, everlasting passion. In many movies, we see couples who are madly in love from start to finish, as if that initial spark never went out. But in real life, passion is just a stage of love. Over time, intense emotion can transform into something calmer and more stable, which doesn't mean that love has disappeared, but rather that it has evolved. Clinging to the idea of everlasting passion can make us feel dissatisfied with relationships that are actually healthy and deep.

Furthermore, romantic love tends to ignore the importance of compatibility and mutual effort. It makes us think that if two people are "meant" to be together, everything will work out automatically. But relationships don't build themselves; they require time, patience, and commitment from both parties. Falling in love is easy, but staying in a healthy relationship is an ongoing process that involves communication, respect, and constant adjustments. Believing in predestined love can cause us to underestimate the work required to maintain a relationship.

The myth also reinforces gender stereotypes. It often portrays women as needing to be rescued by a strong, brave man, while men are seen as heroes who must protect and care for. These ideas are not only outdated, but also harmful, because they limit people to rigid roles that do not always reflect who they really are. In a healthy relationship, both partners are equal and supportive of each other, without falling into stereotypes.

Another misleading aspect of romantic love is the belief that we must sacrifice everything for love. Many stories glorify relationships where people give up their dreams, friendships, or even their identity to be with someone. This can lead us to tolerate toxic relationships or lose sight of what is truly important to us. Loving someone shouldn't mean giving up our essence, but rather finding someone who accepts us and encourages us to be our best selves.

The myth of romantic love also makes us believe that true love is exclusive and that one person should meet all of our emotional needs. In reality, this is neither possible nor fair. People need a support network that includes friends, family, and independent activities. Placing all of our happiness and well-being on one person can be an overwhelming burden on any relationship. It is essential to remember that romantic love is just one part of our lives and should not be our only source of satisfaction.

By debunking the myth of romantic love, we are not saying that love is any less magical or valuable. On the contrary, love is one of the most beautiful and meaningful experiences in life. However, in order to enjoy more fulfilling relationships, it is crucial to approach it with a realistic perspective. Love is not a perfect fantasy or an inevitable destiny, but a conscious choice to care for, respect, and grow with another person.

By leaving behind the myth of romantic love, we open the door to more authentic relationships. We allow ourselves to accept our partners as they are, with their virtues and flaws. We also free ourselves from the pressure of being perfect or finding someone perfect. Instead, we can build relationships based on trust, mutual respect, and shared effort. Because at the end of the day, real love is not the one we find in movies, but the one we create together, day by day.

Self-Love

Self-love is the foundation of any healthy relationship, but it is one of the most misunderstood concepts. We often think that loving ourselves means being selfish, self-centered, or ignoring the needs of others, but that is not the case. Loving others fully and genuinely is only possible when we have learned to love ourselves. It is like trying to fill someone else's glass when our own is empty; you just can't do it. Self-love is not about arrogance, but about recognition, respect, and care for yourself.

Self-love begins with self-knowledge. We cannot love what we do not know. We often live our lives without stopping to reflect on who we really are, what we like, what hurts us, what we need to feel good. This neglect can lead us to rely on others to define us or to fill voids that only we can fill. To practice self-love, it is essential to take the time to know ourselves deeply, accept our strengths and weaknesses, and understand that we are a work in progress, not a finished product.

Accepting our imperfections is an essential step on the path to self-love. We live in a society that bombards us with ideals of perfection in our physicality, emotions, abilities, and even relationships. This pressure can make us feel like we're never enough. But the truth is, no one is perfect, and that's okay. Accepting our flaws doesn't mean settling for them, but understanding that they're part of who we are and that they don't make us any less valuable. By fully accepting ourselves, we create a solid foundation for building more honest relationships free of insecurities.

Taking care of ourselves is another key part of self-love. This includes both physical and emotional care. We often put ourselves at the bottom of the priority list, especially when we're busy caring for others. But we can't be our best selves if we're not well. Exercising, eating healthy, getting enough rest, and taking care of our mental health aren't luxuries—they're necessities. Learning to say no, taking time for ourselves, and setting clear boundaries are acts of self-love that empower us and allow us to be more present for others.

Self-talk is an aspect that we often overlook when we talk about self-love. The way we talk to ourselves can build us up or tear us down. We are often our own worst critic, saying things to ourselves that we would never say to someone we love. Changing that negative self-talk to a positive, compassionate one can completely transform the relationship we have with ourselves. Instead of beating ourselves up for our mistakes, we must learn to forgive ourselves, acknowledge our accomplishments, and speak to ourselves with the same kindness we offer to those we love.

Self-love also means being honest with ourselves about our emotions. Sometimes, instead of facing what we feel, we try to hide or ignore it, thinking that this will make us stronger. But emotions don't just go away because we don't look at them; they tend to build up and, sooner or later, explode. Loving ourselves means allowing ourselves to feel, whether it's joy, sadness, anger, or fear, and finding healthy ways to process those emotions. Acknowledging what we feel doesn't make us weak, it makes us human.

Another important aspect of self-love is recognizing our own worth, regardless of external circumstances. We often tie our self-worth to achievements, material possessions, or the approval of others. When we do this, our happiness and self-love become unstable, because they depend on factors beyond our control. Learning to value who we are, regardless of what we have or what others think, is a profound act of self-love. It frees us from the constant search for external validation and allows us to be more authentic.

Self-love also gives us the courage to walk away from situations and people that don't do us any good. Sometimes we hold on to toxic relationships or environments because we don't think we deserve better or because we're afraid of being alone. But staying in places where we're not respected or valued only drains us emotionally and reinforces the idea that we're not enough. Loving ourselves means recognizing that we deserve relationships and environments that nurture and inspire us, and having the courage to seek out what we truly need.

By practicing self-love, we not only improve our relationship with ourselves, but also with others. When we love ourselves, we are less likely to become emotionally dependent on other people, which reduces the burden we put on our relationships. We are also better able to set healthy boundaries, communicate effectively, and show empathy without losing ourselves in the process. Self-love not only benefits us, but it also improves the quality of our connections with those around us.

Self-love isn't something you achieve overnight; it's an ongoing journey. There will be days when it's easier, and other days when it's challenging. The important thing to remember is that self-love isn't a destination, but rather a daily practice. Every small act of care, every kind word toward ourselves, and every boundary we set are steps on the path to a healthier, more loving relationship with ourselves. And when we learn to love ourselves, we open ourselves up to the possibility of loving and being loved in a more complete and authentic way.

Key To A Deep Connection

The key to a deep connection in any relationship is authenticity, but this authenticity isn't simply being truthful; it's being brave in showing who you really are, with your strengths and your vulnerabilities. Often, we want to connect with someone from a place of perfection, showing only the parts of ourselves that we think will be accepted. However, a deep connection can't come from a place of masks or appearances. Only when both partners feel free to be themselves, without fear of judgment or rejection, can something truly special emerge.

Empathy is another essential component to creating a deep connection. This means not just listening to what the other person is saying, but making an effort to understand what they are feeling. Empathy requires attention, patience, and a willingness to enter another person's world, even if it's different from your own. It's not about always agreeing, but rather validating the other person's emotions and showing that their feelings matter. When someone feels like you truly understand and value them, the bond between you both is strengthened in a unique way.

Open and honest communication is a must. This means speaking clearly about what you feel, what you need, and what you hope for, without expecting the other person to guess what's on your mind. Lack of clear communication can lead to misunderstandings and resentments that erode connection. But communication isn't just about talking; it also involves listening carefully and without interruptions. Often, we're so busy thinking about what we're going to say in response that we don't really hear what's being said to us. Practicing active listening, focusing fully on the other person, is a powerful display of respect and love.

Vulnerability is another key piece in building a deep connection. Opening up to someone and showing your fears, your hurts, and your dreams can be scary, but it's also what allows the other person to truly get close to you. Many times, we try to protect ourselves by building emotional walls, but those walls also block connection. When you allow yourself to be vulnerable, you invite the other person to do the same, creating a safe space where you can both be your authentic selves. Vulnerability is not weakness; it's an act of courage that deepens emotional bonds.

Time and attention are critical to cultivating a deep connection. In modern life, filled with constant distractions, it's easy to be physically present but emotionally absent. However, to build a meaningful relationship, you need to dedicate quality time, without interruptions, to be truly present with the other person. This means turning off your phone, looking into the other person's eyes, and actively engaging in the moment. Connection isn't built overnight; it's a process that requires consistent effort and a sincere investment of time.

Mutual respect is another pillar of a deep connection. This doesn't mean agreeing on everything, but it does mean valuing each other's opinions, feelings, and needs, even when they're different from your own. Respecting someone also includes respecting their boundaries. We often think that the closer we are to someone, the more we can cross certain boundaries, but in reality, respecting those boundaries is what builds trust and allows the relationship to flourish.

Gratitude also plays a big role in connection. It's easy to take the people in our lives for granted, but expressing sincere appreciation for what they do, who they are, and how they contribute to our lives can greatly deepen the relationship. Gratitude doesn't have to be something grand; even small gestures or words of thanks can have a significant impact. When someone feels valued, they're more likely to value and care for the connection between you, too.

A commitment to growing together is another key to deep connection. No relationship remains static; we all change over time, and our relationships must evolve with us. This means being willing to adapt, learn, and work together to overcome challenges. Growing together isn't always easy, but it's what transforms a superficial connection into a relationship that can stand the test of time.

Finally, the key to a deep connection is trust. Without trust, no matter how much love or passion exists, the relationship will be fragile. Trust is built through consistency, honesty, and respect. Every action and word contributes to strengthening or weakening trust. It is important to remember that trust is earned over time, but can be lost in an instant, so we must protect it like a priceless treasure.

A deep connection isn't something that just happens; it's the result of conscious decisions and actions. It requires commitment, effort, and a willingness to be authentic, empathetic, and vulnerable. When we truly open ourselves up to someone and create a space where we can both be ourselves, the connection that emerges is powerful and transformative. Ultimately, a deep connection not only enhances our relationships, but it also enriches us as people.

The Conflict in Love

Conflict in love is inevitable. While the idea of a relationship without disagreements may seem ideal, the reality is that even the happiest couples face differences. But conflict doesn't have to be a negative thing. In fact, it can be an opportunity to strengthen the relationship if it's addressed in a healthy and constructive way. The key is to understand that conflicts are not the problem in and of themselves; what's important is how they're handled.

In love, differences arise because each person has their own set of values, experiences, expectations, and ways of looking at life. These differences can lead to misunderstandings or disagreements when they are not communicated effectively. For example, one person may value time together as their primary love language, while the other may prioritize financial or emotional support. These perspectives are not wrong, they are just different, and that is where conflict can begin.

Conflict can be caused by small things, such as forgetting a special date, or by larger issues, such as disagreements about life plans or core values. However, what's important is not the size of the problem, but how the two people choose to deal with it. Many couples make the mistake of avoiding conflict for fear of hurting the other or damaging the relationship, but this only creates resentment and emotional distance over time. Talking things through, even if it's uncomfortable, is essential to maintaining a healthy relationship.

One of the first things to remember when handling conflict is to stay calm. Arguments tend to escalate when both parties get carried away by emotion and start saying impulsive or hurtful things. In those moments, it's important to stop and remember that the goal isn't to win the argument, but to solve the problem together. A pause to breathe, reflect, and think before speaking can make a big difference in how the conflict plays out.

Clear communication is another key element. Often, arguments go unresolved because people don't express their needs effectively. Instead of blaming or attacking the other person, it's more helpful to speak from a personal perspective, using phrases like "I feel…" or "I need…". For example, instead of saying "You never listen to me," you could say "I feel ignored when I try to share something important and don't get a response." This approach prevents the other person from feeling attacked and opens the door to a more productive conversation.

Listening is just as important as talking. During a conflict, we are often so focused on what we want to say that we don't pay attention to what the other person is trying to communicate. Active listening means being present, not interrupting, and trying to truly understand the other person's point of view. Even if you don't agree, acknowledging what the other person is feeling and validating their emotions can help defuse tension and build a bridge to resolution.

Mutual respect must be maintained at all times. It's easy to get carried away by frustration and resort to name-calling, shouting, or dismissive behavior, but this only destroys trust and increases emotional damage. Even in the most difficult moments of disagreement, it's essential to remember that you're talking to someone you love and respect. Instead of looking for someone to blame, focus on finding solutions.

Forgiveness also plays an important role in conflict resolution. No one is perfect, and everyone makes mistakes. Holding on to resentment only prolongs the pain and makes reconciliation more difficult. Forgiveness doesn't mean forgetting or justifying what happened, but rather deciding not to allow the conflict to continue to affect the relationship. This takes conscious effort and sometimes time, but it's essential to moving forward.

It's important to learn to pick your battles. Not every disagreement deserves to turn into a conflict. Sometimes, the best thing you can do for your relationship is to let small things go that don't have a significant impact. This doesn't mean ignoring your needs or feelings, but rather prioritizing what really matters and avoiding wearing yourself down over trivial things.

Finally, conflicts in love should be seen as an opportunity for growth. Every disagreement is an opportunity to learn more about the other person, their needs, and their limits. It is also an opportunity to reflect on yourself, your reactions, and how you can improve as a couple. Instead of seeing conflict as a threat to the relationship, see it as an opportunity to strengthen it.

Conflict in love is inevitable, but it doesn't have to be destructive. With patience, empathy, and mutual effort, disagreements can become moments of learning and deeper connection. Ultimately, love isn't about avoiding problems, but about facing them together with respect and compromise. When both people work as a team to overcome challenges, the bond becomes stronger and more resilient.

The Difference Between Need and Choice

In love, we often confuse what we need with what we choose. This confusion can lead us to unhealthy relationships or dynamics where we are not truly free to love, but are bound by a sense of lack. Understanding the difference between need and choice is critical to building healthy, fulfilling relationships. This concept may seem simple, but it is deeply rooted in the way we experience our emotions and relate to others.

Neediness is that feeling that we cannot be complete without something or someone. When we feel that we need a person, we give them the power to fill a void in us. This may sound romantic in movies or songs, but in real life it creates a dependency that puts a heavy burden on the relationship. In this state, we look to the other person for solutions to internal problems, such as low self-esteem, fear of loneliness, or emotional insecurity. This is not only unfair to the other person, but it also prevents us from growing as individuals.

On the other hand, choice is a conscious act of wanting to be with someone because we value what that person brings to our lives, not because we need them to feel complete. When we choose to love someone, we do so from a place of abundance, not lack. We don't look to them to save us, validate us, or make us happy. Instead, we recognize our ability to be happy on our own and share that happiness with the other person.

The difference between need and choice is also reflected in how we behave within a relationship. When we love out of need, it is common for possessive or controlling behaviors to emerge. We feel constant fear of losing the other person because we believe that without them we will be incomplete. This can lead to attitudes such as jealousy, emotional manipulation, or even excessive sacrifice of our own needs. This type of love is fragile, because it depends on the other person staying and meeting our expectations, something that is not always possible.

In contrast, when we love from choice, we accept that the other person is free to be with us or not. This love is more secure and mature because it is not based on dependency, but on mutual respect. We know that the other person is with us because they also choose us, and not because they feel obliged or needy. This builds trust and reduces conflicts that arise from insecurities.

It's important to reflect on our own emotions and recognize whether we're acting out of necessity or choice. For example, ask yourself why you want to be with your partner. Is it because you're afraid of being alone? Or because you truly value their company? Identifying these patterns can be uncomfortable, but it's the first step toward building healthier relationships.

One of the biggest obstacles to overcoming neediness is the fear of loneliness. Many people stay in unsatisfying relationships because they can't stand the thought of being alone. But being alone isn't a bad thing. In fact, it can be an opportunity to get to know ourselves better and work on ourselves. When we learn to be okay alone, we stop looking to others for what we can give to ourselves. This allows us to enter into a relationship from a place of strength, not weakness.

Choice also involves accepting the other person as they are, not as we wish they were. When we love out of need, we often try to change the other person to fit our expectations. This creates tension and frustration in the relationship. In contrast, when we choose to love, we accept the other person's imperfections and value their individuality. This doesn't mean we can't express our needs or set boundaries, but we do so from a place of respect and understanding, not demand.

An important point is that neediness doesn't go away overnight. It's a process that requires time, self-exploration, and sometimes professional help. It can be helpful to ask ourselves what voids we're trying to fill with a relationship and how we can work on them on our own. This will not only improve our romantic relationships, but also our relationship with ourselves.

In the end, love based on choice is a freer, more authentic kind of love. It's the kind of love that allows us to grow as people and as a couple, because it's not burdened by unrealistic expectations or irrational fears. Choosing to love someone doesn't mean there will never be challenges or disagreements, but it does mean that we will face those challenges from a place of respect, trust, and mutual commitment.

Understanding the difference between necessity and choice is an act of self-love and love for others. It frees us from the burden of depending on others for our happiness and allows us to build relationships based on true connection and mutual appreciation. When you love from choice, you are not tied to the other person, but you also don't want to leave. It's a daily choice, and that's the foundation of genuine, lasting love.

Keeping the Spark Alive

Keeping the spark alive in a relationship is not something that happens by chance. Although at the beginning of a relationship everything may seem easy and exciting, over time, routine, responsibilities and small differences can wear away at that feeling of newness and excitement. However, it is entirely possible to keep the spark alive if both are willing to work at it consciously. This work does not have to be burdensome or forced, but it does require intention, creativity and, above all, love.

The spark in a relationship is fueled by mutual attention. Often, couples stop paying attention to the small details when they feel comfortable or secure. Those small gestures, like an unexpected text, a sincere compliment, or a lingering hug, are what keep the emotional connection alive. Taking the time to express affection and gratitude, even for the simplest things, can make a big difference. When you show your partner that you value and appreciate them, you strengthen the bond between you.

Another key aspect of keeping the spark alive is open communication. Over time, people change, and it's easy to fall into the trap of assuming you already know everything about your partner. Ask how they're feeling, what their current goals are, what excites them, or what worries them. These conversations not only strengthen the emotional connection, but they also keep the relationship dynamic and interesting. Plus, talking about your own emotions and needs creates a safe space where you both can feel heard and understood.

Spark also depends on the ability to surprise each other. This doesn't mean you should spend money on grand gestures, but find creative ways to break the routine. These can be things as simple as preparing a special dinner at home, planning an unexpected outing, or writing a love note. The key is to show your partner that you are willing to go out of the ordinary to make them feel special.

Quality time is another essential factor. Many couples spend a lot of time together, but they don't necessarily share quality time. Sitting in the same room staring at their phones doesn't count. Plan times where you can both tune out distractions and really be present for each other. This can be a walk together, cooking together, or just sitting down to talk without interruptions. These shared experiences strengthen the connection and create memories you both will cherish.

Keeping the spark alive also involves cultivating physical intimacy. This isn't just about sex, although that's important, but about all the physical gestures that show affection. Hugs, caresses, holding hands, and daily kisses are simple but powerful ways to maintain physical and emotional connection. Never underestimate the power of physical touch to reaffirm love in a relationship.

One aspect that is often overlooked is the importance of maintaining individual interests. While it is crucial to share time and activities with your partner, it is also essential that you both maintain your own passions, friends, and goals. Not only does this give you new topics of conversation, but it also prevents the relationship from becoming stifling. Plus, a person who continues to grow and evolve on their own is much more attractive and stimulating to their partner.

A sense of humor also plays a big role in keeping the spark alive. Laughing together creates a special connection and helps relieve stress. Find time to enjoy things that make you laugh, like watching a funny movie, remembering funny stories, or even joking around with each other. Laughter is a reminder that despite the challenges, you can enjoy life together.

Another important component is handling conflict in a healthy way. Arguments and disagreements are inevitable in any relationship, but how you handle them can make the difference between strengthening or weakening the spark. Approach problems respectfully and look for solutions instead of blaming each other. When you face challenges as a team, you strengthen your connection and trust in each other.

Finally, it's important to remember why you fell in love in the first place. Talk about happy memories, look back at old photos, or even revisit places that marked important moments in your relationship. These actions help you reconnect with the positive emotions of the beginning and remember that the spark is still there, even though it can sometimes get buried under the demands of everyday life.

Keeping the spark alive isn't something that happens automatically, but it's not an impossible job either. It requires small, consistent efforts, but these efforts are what make a relationship special and long-lasting. When you both commit to taking care of that spark, you not only keep the magic alive, but you also build a stronger, deeper love over time. In the end, the spark is a reflection of the love, attention, and effort you both put into the relationship. And that's something worth taking care of.

Overcoming Mistakes and Rebuilding Trust

Overcoming mistakes and rebuilding trust in a relationship is one of the most difficult tests a couple can face. Mistakes, whether small oversights or major betrayals, have the power to break something as delicate as trust. But while it is a difficult path, it is not impossible. If both people are willing to work at it, trust can be rebuilt and the relationship can come out even stronger than it was before.

The first step to getting over a mistake is to honestly acknowledge it. When someone makes a mistake in a relationship, it can be tempting to minimize it, justify it, or even avoid talking about it. However, this only deepens the wound. Accepting full responsibility for the mistake is crucial. This involves clearly stating what you did wrong and showing that you understand how it affected your partner. Words like "I'm sorry" carry weight only if they are accompanied by genuine reflection and a change in behavior.

On the other hand, it is essential that the person affected also allows him or herself to feel his or her emotions. It is normal to feel anger, sadness, confusion or even a mixture of all these emotions. Repressing what is felt only prolongs the healing process. If you are on the side of the one who was hurt, give yourself permission to process what happened. And if you are on the side of the one who made the mistake, it is important to be patient and allow your partner to express what he or she feels without interrupting him or trying to rush the reconciliation.

Open communication is key to beginning to heal. Talking about the problem can be uncomfortable, but ignoring it or sweeping it under the rug only creates a greater distance between the two of you. It is important that both parties sit down to talk honestly and respectfully. Listening without interrupting, asking questions to better understand how the other feels, and avoiding blame or attacks are fundamental elements to moving forward. Although the conversation can be painful, it is the first step to begin to build a new understanding.

Rebuilding trust also involves consistent actions. Words are important, but actions are what really show that someone is committed to not repeating the mistake. If you promise to change a behavior, you must be willing to show with your actions that you are doing so. This can include simple things like being more transparent, setting clear boundaries, or avoiding situations that could put the relationship at risk. Consistency is what allows trust to grow back over time.

Forgiveness plays a crucial role in this process. But it's important to understand that forgiveness doesn't happen immediately, nor can it be forced. To forgive, the hurt person needs time to process what happened, and the person who made the mistake needs to show patience. Forgiveness doesn't mean forgetting the mistake or acting like it didn't happen, but rather accepting that it happened and deciding not to let it control the relationship in the future. It's an act of liberation, both for the hurt person and the person seeking to make amends.

However, it is crucial to recognize that forgiveness and rebuilding trust do not always guarantee that the relationship will continue. There are mistakes that, by their nature, may be too difficult to overcome. If that is the case, it is also valid to decide to end the relationship, as long as this decision is made from a place of reflection and not impulse. In those cases, the healing process continues, but on an individual basis.

Another important aspect is to avoid unrealistic expectations. Broken trust cannot be repaired overnight. It requires time, effort, and ongoing commitment from both parties. It is not about "going back to the way things were," because the relationship will inevitably change. Instead, the goal should be to build something new, stronger, and more honest. This approach helps avoid frustrations and allows both parties to focus on the small steps forward.

Finally, overcoming mistakes and rebuilding trust can also be an opportunity to grow together. This process can bring to light underlying issues that you may not have faced before, and by addressing them, you can strengthen your relationship. It also teaches you to communicate better, be more empathetic, and value what you have more. Relationships aren't perfect because people aren't, but when you're both willing to learn from mistakes, you can find a deeper, more mature love.

Overcoming mistakes and rebuilding trust isn't easy. It requires honesty, patience, communication, and a genuine willingness to heal and grow. But when you're both committed to working together, the process becomes a path to a more authentic and resilient relationship. In the end, the most important thing to remember is that love isn't just a feeling, but also a daily decision to choose the other person, even when things aren't perfect. If you both choose to work on it, broken trust can be transformed into a stronger bridge that unites you.

Love in Modern Times

Love in modern times is experienced in ways our past generations could not have imagined. Technology, social media, and fast-paced living have transformed the way we meet, connect, and maintain relationships with others. While the foundations of love—connection, respect, and commitment—remain the same, the paths to them have profoundly changed. Navigating love in this modern world can be exciting, but it also poses unique challenges worth exploring.

One of the biggest changes in how we experience love has to do with how we meet people. In the past, relationships often took place within close social circles, whether in the neighborhood, at work, or at community activities. Today, dating apps and online platforms have opened up a whole new world. You can meet someone who lives miles away, who has completely different interests than you, or who you might never have encountered in your everyday life. While this connectivity is wonderful, it can also be overwhelming. Having so many options can make us feel unsure about whether we are choosing correctly or whether there is someone "better" out there to discover.

Social media has also changed the dynamics of love. It's now common to share personal moments with the world, from couple photos to anniversaries and engagements. While this can be a cute way to celebrate love, it can also create unnecessary pressure. It's easy to fall into the game of comparing yourself to other couples, wondering if your relationship is romantic, exciting, or happy enough like the ones you see on Instagram. But what we must not forget is that social media is just a carefully curated window. No one shows the arguments, disagreements, or moments of doubt that are a natural part of any relationship.

Another important aspect of love in modern times is the impact of instant communication. Thanks to smartphones, it is now possible to stay in touch with your partner anytime, anywhere. This has obvious advantages, such as the ability to stay connected even from a distance. However, it can also lead to unrealistic expectations. Sometimes, feeling like you have to respond immediately to a message can become a source of stress. Constant availability can cause us to forget the importance of setting healthy boundaries and respecting the moments when each person needs their personal space.

The speed at which we live also affects how we experience love. In a world where everything seems to move quickly, from jobs to news, it can be easy to fall into the trap of seeking instant gratification in our relationships. We want things to flow smoothly, for everything to be perfect right away, and sometimes we give up at the first hurdle. But love requires patience and consistent work. Building a strong relationship takes time, and this means accepting that not everything will be perfect from the start.

In addition, expectations about relationships have evolved. In the past, many people sought to fulfill traditional roles as a couple. Today, relationships are built on equality, mutual understanding, and individuality. This change is positive, as it fosters more balanced and respectful relationships.

However, it can also be tricky to find the right balance between maintaining a strong connection with your partner while also retaining your own identity. Modern love requires us to understand that being independent and being in a relationship are not opposites, but rather complementary.

A particular challenge of modern love is dealing with constant distractions. Phones, social media, and work demands can make it difficult to fully focus on our partner. Spending quality time together can feel more complicated than ever. But this difficulty also teaches us an important lesson: love cannot be automatic or secondary. It requires conscious effort. Turning off your phone during dinner or setting aside time to talk uninterrupted are small acts that can make a big difference.

Love in modern times also invites us to reflect on the meaning of intimacy. Even though we are more connected than ever, many people report feeling lonely in their relationships. This is because intimacy is not just about sharing physical space or quick messages, but about sharing thoughts, emotions, and dreams. Creating a safe space where both partners can be authentic is crucial for a relationship to flourish in this world full of noise.

Finally, modern love reminds us of the importance of adapting. Relationships, like everything in life, are subject to change. This doesn't mean that their foundations change, but the circumstances around them evolve. Learning to adapt to new jobs, moves, global crises, or personal changes is essential to maintaining a strong connection. In a world that is constantly changing, love must also be flexible and resilient.

Love in modern times is a reflection of our times: complicated, fast-paced, sometimes confusing, but always full of possibilities. Although the challenges are different than in generations past, the desire to love and be loved remains the same. With awareness, patience, and genuine commitment, it is possible to navigate love in this modern world and build relationships that are truly worthwhile. The secret is to not let distractions, societal expectations, or technologies dominate what really matters: human connection.

Maintaining Our Identity in Love

When we fall in love, it's natural to want to share everything with the other person. Suddenly, our lives seem to become intertwined, and that desire to be together can be so strong that we let our personal identity fade into the relationship. However, maintaining our identity in love is not only essential to our emotional well-being, but also to the health of the relationship itself. A strong, long-lasting relationship is not made up of two people losing themselves in each other, but of two complete individuals choosing to be together.

Maintaining our identity begins with knowing ourselves well. Before we can share our life with someone else, we need to be clear about who we are, what we like, what values we have, and what goals we want to achieve. A relationship should not become an excuse to put aside our passions or our dreams. On the contrary, it should be a space where we can grow and feel supported in what makes us unique.

It's easy to fall into the trap of adapting too much to our partner. We want to please them, make them happy, avoid conflict. This can lead us to say yes to things we don't really want to do or to accept changes that don't represent us. For example, if you've always loved going for walks alone in the mornings, but you stop doing it because your partner prefers to have breakfast together at that time, you might feel like you're giving up an important part of yourself. While compromise is a natural part of any relationship, we shouldn't confuse compromise with giving up. Your needs and desires matter too, and finding a balance is key.

Another important aspect of maintaining our identity is maintaining our relationships and activities outside of a relationship. Often, when we start a relationship, we tend to spend less time with friends or family, or give up hobbies we used to enjoy. While this may seem harmless at first, in the long run it can leave us feeling disconnected from ourselves. Continuing to cultivate friendships, keep in touch with family, and spend time on activities that make us happy is essential to feeling fulfilled. It's not a betrayal of your partner to make time for these things; it's a way to nurture your emotional well-being.

Open communication is essential when it comes to maintaining our identity in a relationship. Talking to your partner about your needs, your boundaries, and what makes you feel good can prevent misunderstandings. For example, if you need time to yourself after a stressful day, it's important to express that rather than forcing yourself to be available if you really need that personal space. A partner who loves and respects you will understand that taking care of yourself benefits the relationship as well.

One of the biggest risks of losing our identity in a relationship is that it can lead to resentment. If you're constantly sacrificing your wants or needs to please your partner, you're likely to eventually feel frustrated or dissatisfied. This can create tensions that, over time, can erode the connection. Staying true to yourself not only protects you, but the relationship as well. A partner who sees that you're authentic will also feel more comfortable being authentic with you.

Sometimes, fear of conflict leads us to put our identity aside. We worry about not appearing selfish or not wanting to cause trouble. However, being honest about who you are and what you need is not selfish; it is an act of self-love. In fact, a healthy relationship does not fear conflict. Differences of opinion are normal, and learning to handle them respectfully is a sign of maturity and commitment. Standing up for your identity does not mean imposing yourself on your partner, but rather finding ways to coexist that work for both of you.

It's also important to remember that our identities evolve over time. Experiences, goals, and circumstances change, and that's okay. The challenge in a relationship is to adapt to these changes while still being who we are. This requires flexibility and constant communication. If something you used to enjoy no longer fulfills you, talk about it. If you're exploring new passions or interests, share them. Growing as an individual doesn't mean you're leaving your partner behind, but rather you're enriching the relationship with new perspectives and experiences.

Lastly, it's essential that you not only maintain your identity, but that you also support your partner in doing the same. The strongest relationships are those where both people feel free to be who they are without fear of judgment or disapproval. Celebrate their differences, encourage their passions, and respect their boundaries. This creates a space where both of you can flourish, both together and individually.

Maintaining our identity in love is no easy task, especially when we are immersed in the excitement of a relationship. However, it is a worthwhile effort. Being yourself not only allows you to enjoy the relationship more, but it also ensures that you are building something real and lasting. After all, true love does not require us to give up who we are, but rather invites us to be fully ourselves alongside someone who values us for it.

Evolving Together

Love is not a static state. It is something that evolves over time, just like the people involved in the relationship. This means that not only does the relationship change, but so does each individual within it. Understanding and accepting this reality is essential to maintaining a healthy, long-lasting connection. Evolving together doesn't mean that you're always on the same page or that you never face challenges, but that you're both willing to adapt, learn, and grow as a team.

When a relationship first begins, everything seems exciting and fresh. It's easy to feel like nothing will ever change, that you'll always be those happy, connected people. However, life has a way of challenging that illusion. Over the years, we face personal, professional, and emotional changes. Maybe one of you decides to change careers, or perhaps health issues arise, or even something as simple as developing new interests. These changes may seem like threats to the balance of the relationship, but they're actually opportunities to strengthen the bond if you're both willing to evolve together.

Evolving together begins with accepting that change is inevitable. Often, people fear change because they associate it with loss. If my partner is no longer the same person I knew, does that mean the love is over? The answer is no. Change doesn't have to be a negative thing. In fact, it can be a sign of growth and maturity. The important thing is to be willing to get to know each other again and again, because the person you love today won't be exactly the same in five or ten years. And that's okay.

A key aspect of evolving together is communication. We can't expect our partner to understand what we're going through or how we're changing if we don't tell them. Talking openly and honestly about our feelings, fears, and hopes creates a space where you can both share your evolution without fear of being judged. Maybe you're starting to get interested in something new, or maybe you're dealing with an insecurity that wasn't there before. Saying it out loud not only helps your partner understand you, but it also fosters a deeper connection.

Another essential component is mutual support. Evolving together doesn't mean that you both have to change at the same pace or in the same way. Sometimes, one of you will be facing a more intense period of transformation, while the other will be in a more stable stage. At those times, support is crucial. For example, if your partner is considering going back to school after years of being in the same job, she may feel scared or insecure. Supporting her, even if it means adjusting your routines or taking on more temporary responsibilities, shows that you are committed to her growth.

Evolving together also involves learning to negotiate differences. You won't always agree on how to handle changes or where you want to go as a couple. These differences can be challenging, but they don't have to be destructive. The key is to listen with empathy, look for common ground, and be willing to compromise when necessary. For example, if one of you wants to move to a new city for work but the other isn't sure, instead of seeing it as a conflict, it can be an opportunity to explore together what really matters to both of you and find a solution that works.

It's also important to stay curious about your partner. Over time, it's easy to assume that you already know everything about the other person. But if you're both growing and changing, there's always something new to discover. Ask questions, be interested in what they're learning or experiencing, and share your own new insights. This curiosity keeps the relationship fresh and helps prevent it from becoming monotonous.

Growing together won't always be easy. There will be times when one of you feels lost or even questions whether the relationship can survive the changes. These moments of doubt are normal and don't mean the relationship is doomed. In fact, overcoming these challenges together can make your bond stronger. The key is to be willing to work as a team and remember that love isn't something that just happens; it's something that's built day by day.

Finally, evolving together also means celebrating mutual achievements. Every small step toward growth, whether individually or as a couple, deserves to be recognized. Maybe one of you managed to overcome a fear, or you both found a new way to resolve a conflict. These moments are reminders that, despite the challenges, you are moving in the right direction. Celebrating them not only strengthens the connection, but also fuels the motivation to continue growing together.

Evolving together is not a destination, but rather an ongoing journey. It is a process of adapting, supporting, and rediscovering each other over and over again. In the end, what matters is not whether you always agree or whether everything is perfect, but that you are both committed to walking that path, with its ups and downs, as a team. Because in true love, growing doesn't mean growing apart, but rather finding ways to get even closer, even as you both change.

www.ingramcontent.com/pod-product-compliance
Lightning Source LLC
Chambersburg PA
CBHW051902130726
47987CB00002B/941